Level B

Math Word Problems

Decimals and Percents

SERIES TITLES

Math Word Problems—Whole Numbers and Fractions
Math Word Problems—Decimals and Percents
Math Word Problems—Mixed Concepts: Whole Numbers to Percents

Anita Harnadek

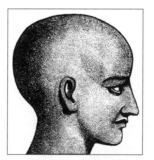

© 1996, 1979
CRITICAL THINKING BOOKS & SOFTWARE
www.CriticalThinking.com
P.O. Box 448 • Pacific Grove • CA 93950-0448
Phone 800-458-4849 • FAX 831-393-3277
ISBN 0-89455-821-8
Printed in the United States of America

Contents

About This Book

The word problems in a general math textbook are almost always grouped so that the student merely has to use the same operation or solution technique for all problems in a group in order to get the answers. What the student needs, and what this book gives, are problems which are arranged so that they cannot be solved by rote processes, which are arranged so that thought and understanding are required. At the same time, we do not want to give word problems which leave students lost in a confusing maze of words and ideas without any clue of how to take a first step toward solving the problem.

We want students to learn when and how to apply their arithmetic knowledge to solving word problems and later to real-life situations, but once the basic concepts are taught, it can be frustrating to search for word problems that fill these needs. Teachers are always looking for word problems that meet the following criteria:

1. The word problems must be at the arithmetic level of the student.

2. They must be at (or below) the reading level of the student.

3. They must be clearly stated.

4. They should be arithmetically mixed so that the student does not automatically add (or divide in a certain order or subtract or whatever) the numbers given in order to get the answer.

5. They should, at least for the most part, be real-life problems requiring practical applications of arithmetic.

The word problems in this book satisfy the above criteria. Designed to spare the teacher the time and trouble of trying to find or create more word problems, and designed to provide the students with practice using various operations with a particular concept or with practice using various operations with various concepts, the problems allow you to give your students the kinds of practice problems they need.

All problems are nongraded in content and are written at an elementary reading level, making them suitable for students at any grade level who have been taught the four basic arithmetic operations.

These problems allow students to use a variety of arithmetic skills in a variety of contexts to solve problems. The result is that the students really learn when and how to apply their arithmetic knowledge to life situations.

And this is what learning arithmetic is all about, isn't it?

Instructions

Instructions are provided at the beginning of each section. The example problems provided in the instructions can be used as models for solving the problems and to reassure students about what is expected of them in solving the word problems.

Answers for all problems are provided at the back of the book.

About Introductory Word Problems

I have found that it can be frustrating to try to teach students to use common sense in solving word problems. You read a problem with the students, and you ask leading questions to try to get them to reason out the answer. Just as you think you're making progress, they ask, "I don't see what all that stuff has to do with it. All I wanna know is, do I add, subtract, multiply, or divide to get the answer?"

It seems the students know they need

arithmetic practice and they don't mind that so much, but they can't see why it should be messed up by surrounding it with a lot of words. That is, they seem to think that the purpose of a word problem is to give them more arithmetic practice, rather than to teach them how to apply what they already know.

This first section is especially designed for such students, as well as for students who either have not done word problems before or who freeze at the sight of a word problem.

To assist these students, the problems in this section all use the same numbers—10 and 40. All answers are $\frac{1}{4}$, $\frac{3}{4}$, 3, 4, 30, 50, or 400. The idea is to make it obvious that the problems are not supposed to provide arithmetic practice, thus allowing students to concentrate on what is being asked and on how to reason out the answers rather than worry about manipulating the numbers afterwards.

The hope is that once the students gain confidence in their abilities to understand, break down, and solve word problems by experiencing success with the problems in this section, they can then move without fear to problems which require both reasoning ability and arithmetic ability.

About Decimals

Some problems use whole numbers but have decimal answers; some problems use decimals but have whole-number answers; and sometimes both the problems and the answers are in decimals. The students are told to carry a decimal answer to two places (converting decimals beyond two places into a two-place decimal plus a fraction) unless the answer has only one decimal place. It is assumed that the students know how to work with fractions.

All answers given are exact. Again, if you would rather have your students give approximate answers for some problems, or if you would rather have your students carry the decimal answers to more or fewer places, feel free to do so.

You may wonder why problems were not chosen so that the answers came out "better"—e.g., so that money problems came out with whole cents or speed problems came out with whole mph or kph. The reason they were not so chosen is that everyday life problems come out with "sloppy" answers more often than not, and our teaching the students in school how to cope with such answers will prepare them for the answers they'll get when they start applying what they've learned.

It is important that the students pay attention to what is being asked. Two problems which may seem to have the same answer may have different answers. For example, "Peas sell at 3 cans for $1. (a) You buy 3 cans of them. How much does each can of peas cost you? (b) You buy only one can of them. How much do you pay?" The answer to (a) is $33\frac{1}{3}$ ¢, and the answer to (b) is 34¢.

As in previous sections, problems requiring knowledge of everyday units of measure are interspersed throughout other problems.

About Percents 1

Students who can work with fractions and decimals still have an inordinate amount of trouble with percents. They can answer the questions, "What decimal is $\frac{3}{4}$?" and, "What percent is .75?" and yet not be able to write $\frac{3}{4}$ as a percent. They can know that .2 = 20%. They can work with the problem, "80% of what number is 40?" and can know that 100 – 20 = 80 and yet not have any idea of how to solve the problem, "Jackson paid $40 for a jacket which was on sale for 20% off. What was the regular price of the jacket?" (How many students would solve that problem by taking 20% of $40 = $8, and concluding erroneously that the regular price must be $40 + $8 = $48?!)

The problems in this section present many everyday situations. Each situation is approached from more than one viewpoint. For example, if a 20% discount is being offered, one problem states the regular price and asks several questions, while another problem states the discounted price and asks analogous questions. A third problem states both the selling price and the discounted price and asks, among other things, the percent of the discount.

This section assumes that the students can work with both fractions and decimals. But since this section is meant to be used by students who need a better basic understanding of percents, it avoids, for the most part, fractional percents. It is hoped that the repetitive nature of the problems will help the students learn to work accurately and comfortably with basic percent problems and to have a better understanding of exactly what percents are all about.

Once your students have mastered the problems in this section, they should be ready to try the problems in the next section.

About Percents 2

Although students are instructed to write a non-whole-percent answer as a mixed number rather than as a decimal, the contexts in some problems (such as problems 5 and 16) indicate that decimal percents may be acceptable answers. In such cases, accept either a decimal or a fraction answer. (If you would like your students to write all non-whole-number answers as decimals—e.g., 87.5%, not $87\frac{1}{2}$ %—feel free to change the instructions.)

Also, all answers given are exact. If you feel at times that you would rather have your students give approximate answers, there is no reason not to do this.

1. Introductory Word Problems

INSTRUCTIONS

A. No problem is meant to trick you.

Example

Problem: Darby walked 40 miles at an average rate of 10 miles an hour. How many hours did he walk?

Answer: 4 (Assume the only walking he did was the 40 miles stated in the problem.)

B. No information is missing.

Example

Problem: Ten people ate a total of 40 hamburgers at a party. How many hamburgers did each person eat?

Answer: 4 (It is obvious that we cannot answer the question unless we assume either that the hamburgers were shared equally among the 10 people or that the average number of hamburgers per person is wanted. Since we are told that no information is missing, we assume either or both of these things, and we get an answer of 4.)

C. If the answer is a fraction, write it in reduced form.

Example

Problem: Forty people shared 10 pies. How much did each person get?

Answer: $\frac{1}{4}$ pie (We get an answer of $\frac{10}{40}$ pie, which we reduce to $\frac{1}{4}$ pie.)

1. On the way to Big City, Ilson drove at an average rate of 10 mph. On the way back, she drove at an average rate of 40 mph. How much faster was her rate on the way back than on the way going?

2. On the way to Big City, Ilson drove 10 miles. She took the long way coming back and drove 40 miles. How many miles did she drive on the round trip?

3. Ilson rode her bicycle 10 kilometers to Big City on each of 40 days. How many kilometers did she ride?

4. Ilson drove 40 kilometers yesterday and 10 kilometers today. How far did she drive in the two days?

5. Ilson is going on a 40-kilometer drive. She has driven 10 kilometers so far. How many more 10-kilometer legs does she need to drive in order to finish her trip?

6.   Ilson drove 40 kilometers to Big City and 10 kilometers to Midville. How many kilometers did she drive?

7.   Young bought a pair of shoes for $10. She bought another pair of shoes for $40. How much were the two pairs of shoes?

8.   Young bought shoes for $40 at a price of $10 a pair. How many pairs of shoes did she buy?

9.   Young owns a shoe store. She bought 40 pairs of shoes at $10 a pair. How much did she pay for these shoes?

10.   Young bought a pair of shoes for $10. She started with $40. How many more pairs of the same kind of shoes can she buy?

11. Young thought the price of a new pair of shoes would be $10, but the shoes cost $40. By how much was her estimate off?

12. Young owns a shoe store. She sold 40 pairs of shoes at a profit of $10 a pair. How much profit did she make from these sales?

13. Young sold 10 pairs of shoes for a total profit of $40. What was her profit per pair?

14. Sharon used to be 10 years old. Now she is 40.
  a. How much younger did she used to be than she is now?

  b. How much older is she now than she used to be?

  c. How many years has it been since she was 10 years old?

15. Each of 10 people is 40 years old. What is the sum of their ages?

16. Sharon is now 10 years old. How many more decades does she have to go in order to be 40 years old?

17. Sharon used to be 10 years old. Now she is 40 years old. How many times as old is she now as when she was 10?

18. Forty years ago Sharon was 10 years old. How old is she now?

19. Olsen went on a diet to lose 40 pounds. He has lost 10 pounds so far. What fraction of the 40 pounds has he lost so far?

20.   Each person on a diet lost 10 pounds. The total weight lost was 40 pounds. How many people were on the diet?

21.   Olsen wanted to lose 40 pounds. He has lost 10 pounds in the first month of the diet. At this rate, how many more months will it take him to lose the desired weight?

22.   Olsen went on a diet to lose 40 pounds. He has lost 10 pounds so far. How much does he still have to lose to reach his goal?

23.   Ten people went on a diet, each hoping to lose 40 pounds. How much weight do the 10 people hope to lose?

24.   Ten people on diets have lost a total of 40 pounds. What is the average weight loss per person?

25. Olsen went on a diet. He lost 40 pounds in the first twelve weeks. He lost 10 pounds in the next six weeks. How much did he lose in the eighteen weeks?

26. You bought one share of stock for $10. You bought another share of stock for $40. How much did you pay for the two shares of stock?

27. You bought some stock for $10 a share. It is now worth $40 a share. How much more is it worth now?

28. You bought 10 shares of stock at $40 a share. How much did you pay?

29. You paid $40 for stock at $10 a share. How many shares did you buy?

30. You had $40. You bought one share of stock for $10. How many more shares of this stock can you buy?

31. You bought 40 shares of stock at $10 a share. How much did you pay?

32. It took you 40 minutes to do the first 20 problems on a test. It took you 10 minutes to do the other problems on the test. How much time did you take to do the test?

33. Yesterday you did 40 problems in 30 minutes. Today you did 10 problems of the same kind in 30 minutes. How many more problems did you do yesterday than today in 30 minutes?

34. You have spent 40 minutes on each of 10 tests in the past two weeks. How much time have you spent on tests in this time?

35. You are doing a 40-problem test. You have finished the first 10 problems in just one minute. At this rate, in how many more minutes will you finish the test?

36. Yesterday you did 40 problems in 30 minutes. Today you did 10 problems in 30 minutes. How many problems did you do in the 60 minutes?

37. You did 40 problems in 10 minutes. How many problems did you do on average in each minute?

38. You got 10 problems wrong on a 40-problem test.
   a. What fraction of the problems did you get wrong?

   b. What fraction of the problems did you get right?

39. You got 10 problems wrong on a 40-problem test. How many problems did you get right?

40.   During the past three weeks, you have done all the problems on 10 tests. There were 40 problems on each test. How many problems did you do?

41.   You took 40 minutes to finish a test. You took 10 minutes for each section of the test. How many sections did the test have?

42.   You took a 40-problem test. You couldn't do 10 of the problems. How many problems could you do?

43.   A two-part test has 40 problems in one section. The other section has 10 problems. How many problems are on the test?

44.   Bart was learning to use a meter stick. He measured 10 different things at a total of 40 meters. Each thing measured was the same length. How long was each thing?

45. Bart was learning to use a meter stick. He had something 40 meters long to measure. He measured 10 meters of it and then got tired.

   a. What fraction of the job had he done?

   b. What fraction of the job did he still have left to do?

   c. How many more times does he have to measure 10 meters of the thing in order to finish the job?

46. Bart was learning to use a meter stick. He measured the depth of the yard at 10 meters. The yard was really 40 meters deep. By how much was Bart off?

47. Each of 10 students measured a distance of 40 meters. What was the total distance measured by these students?

48. The telephone company billed 40 customers for $10 each. What was the total billing?

49.   Your telephone bill this month was $40. Last month it was $10. How much more was your bill this month than last month?

50.   Your telephone bill this month was $40. Last month it was $10. How much was it for the two months?

51.   During the last 10 months, you spent $40 making telephone calls. What was the average amount you spent each month for calls?

52.   Your telephone bill has been $40 a month for the last 10 months. How much has your total bill been for these months?

53.   Your telephone bill last month was $40. You have paid $10 of it. How many more times do you have to pay $10 in order to pay the bill in full?

54.   A teacher needed 10 students for one project and 40 students for another project. How many times greater than the number needed for the first project was the difference in the number of students needed for the two projects?

55.   A teacher needed 10 students for a project, and 40 students volunteered to help. How many more volunteered than were needed?

56.   A teacher needs 40 students for projects, and 10 students are needed for each project. How many projects are there?

57.   A teacher needed 10 students for one project and 40 students for another project. How many students were needed for these projects?

58.   Forty students volunteered for projects. The teacher used 10 students on each project. Each student was used exactly once. How many projects were there?

59.   A teacher needed 40 students for each of 10 projects. How many students were needed?

60.   You had $40. You paid $10 for a case of paper. How many more cases of paper can you buy?

61.   Paper used to sell for $10 a case. Now it is $40 a case. How much more is it now than it used to be?

62.   Paper sells for $10 a case at one place. At another place it sells for $40 a case. If you buy the paper at the first place, how many more cases could you get for $40 than you could get if you buy it at the second place?

63.   Paper sells for $10 a case at one place. At another place it sells for $40 a case. You buy a case from each place. How much do you spend?

2. Decimals

INSTRUCTIONS

A. Do not round off any answer unless the problem makes it right to do so.

Example

Problem: Peas sell at 3 cans for $1.01. You buy one can of peas. How much will you be charged?

Answer: $.34 or 34¢ (You can't pay a store a fractional part of one cent.)

B. For part of a dollar, carry the answer to two decimal places. Do not show decimal places for cents.

Example

Problem: You buy 3 cans of peas for $1.01. What is the average price of one of these cans of peas?

Answer: $.33$\frac{2}{3}$ or 33$\frac{2}{3}$ ¢ (not 33.66$\frac{2}{3}$ ¢)

C. Suppose an answer is a dollar or more. Then write it as dollars.

Example

Problem: Peas sell at 50¢ a can. How much will 4 cans of peas cost?

Answer: $2 or $2.00 (not 200¢)

D. No problem is meant to trick you.

Example

Problem: You buy meat for $3.87 and give the cashier $5. How much change do you get?

Answer: $1.13 (Assume you pay the full price for the meat. Assume you don't buy anything else. Assume there is no sales tax. Assume you get the correct change.)

E. Assume that a business will round up, not down, when you are to pay. (Note that gas stations are an exception to this rule. The price on the pump is rounded in the usual arithmetic way.)

Example

Problem: Peas sell at 3 cans for $1. You buy one can of peas. How much will you be charged?

Answer: $.34 or 34¢ (not $.33 or 33¢)

F. If an answer is not about money and if the problem does not tell you how many decimal places to use, then carry the division to two decimal places unless you have a zero remainder before then.

Example

Problem: Write $\frac{5}{2}$ as a decimal.

Answer: 2.5 (not 2.50)

Example

Problem: Write $\frac{49}{16}$ as a decimal.

Answer: $3.06\frac{1}{4}$ (not $3\frac{1}{16}$, not $3.0\frac{5}{8}$, not $3.062\frac{1}{2}$, and not 3.0625)

Example

Problem: Compute $\frac{49}{16}$ to three decimal places.

Answer: $3.062\frac{1}{2}$

1. Gasoline sells for 90.6¢ a half-gallon. How much will 6 gallons cost?

2. You buy meat for $5.88 and bread for 65¢. How much do you spend?

3. What is the average of 3, 5, 7, and 8?

4. It takes Bart 1.6 times as long to do a job as it takes you. You can do the job in 35 minutes. How long does it take Bart to do the job?

5. It takes Marty 1.4 times as long to do a job as it takes you. Marty can do the job in 35 minutes. How long does it take you to do the job?

6. Ms. Galloway's gross pay last week was $325.75. The payroll office deducted the following: $19.87 for social security tax, $74.92 for federal income tax, $16.29 for state income tax, $10.50 for union dues, and $11 for miscellaneous. How much will Ms. Galloway's paycheck be?

7. In baseball, a batting average is figured by dividing the number of times at bat into the number of hits. The answer is rounded to three decimal places.
    a. Royer had 3 hits in 10 times at bat. What was his batting average?

    b. Jefferson had 4 hits in 11 times at bat. What was his batting average?

    c. Timons had 6 hits in 19 times at bat. What was his batting average?

8. a. Write 8 ounces as a number of pounds.

    b. Write 17 ounces as a number of pounds.

    c. Write 7.6 pounds as number of ounces.

9. Peaches sell at 5 cans for $1.76. You buy just one can of them. How much are you charged?

10. Mr. Thompson earns $420.21 a week.
    a. How much is this a year?

    b. How much is this a month?

11. At the end of the semester, Robin owed book fines of $4.35 and lab fees of $2.30. She paid both. She started with $10. How much should she have left?

12. On his fifth birthday, Charles was 1.3 meters tall. The next year he grew 6 centimeters. The following year he grew 8 centimeters. How tall was he on his seventh birthday?

13. Brad counts up his loose change. He has 10 quarters, 4 dimes, 7 nickels, and 14 pennies. What is the total?

14. Paula bought a book for $6.75, paper for $4.78, and pens for $1.76.
    a. How much did she spend?

    b. She started out with $15.32. How much should she have left?

15. Last year Ms. Trent earned $15,675. This year she will earn $20,250. How many times higher will her income this year be than her income last year?

16. Gasoline sells for 93.7¢ a half-gallon. How much will 14.7 gallons cost?

17. Gasoline sells for 92.4¢ a half-gallon. How many gallons will $4 buy?

18. You buy 8 records for $4.67 each. How much do you spend?

19. Ms. Dawson priced a new car at one dealer at $5,567.29. She priced the same kind of car at another dealer at $5,329.48. Which dealer had the higher price, and how much higher was it?

20. A map uses a scale of 1.5 cm = 10 km. The distance between two cities is really 57 km. How far apart will they be on the map?

21.   **a.**   Write 9 inches as a number of feet.

b.   Write 8 inches as a number of feet.

c.   Write 3.4 feet as a number of inches.

22. Mrs. Unser bought 5 pounds of potatoes at 35¢ a pound. She also bought a dozen oranges at 3 for 28¢.

    a. How much were the potatoes?

    b. How much were the oranges?

    c. How much was the total?

    d. She gave the cashier $10. How much change did she get?

23. What is the average of 2.9, 5.4, and 7.6?

24. Mr. Clark earns $18,750.16 a year. On the average, how much is this a week?

25. Mrs. Clark earns $415.35 a week. How much is this a year?

26.   Gasoline sells for 93.7¢ a half-gallon.
    a.   You buy 7.5 gallons. How much are you charged?

    b.   You buy 7.6 gallons. How much are you charged?

27.   You buy 3 pairs of gloves. The first pair costs $5.87. The second pair costs $9.58. The third pair costs $12.96.
    a.   How much altogether do you spend?

    b.   On the average, what is the cost of each pair of gloves you buy?

    c.   You started out with $30. How much should you have left?

28.   You buy 5 records for $5.68 each. You also buy 6 records for $1.39 each. How much do you spend?

29. A fire station sold 38,469 raffle tickets on a new car. The tickets were $1.50 each.
   a. How much did the fire station collect?

   b. They paid $5,800 for the new car they gave away. How much profit did they make?

30. Melissa bought a loaf of bread for 64¢, a dozen eggs for $1.29, and a dozen oranges at 3 for 55¢. She gave the cashier a $10 bill. How much change did she get?

31. Daily News has a circulation of 45,875. Daily Times has a circulation of 58,754. How many times higher is the circulation of Daily Times than that of Daily News?

32. Ms. Norton earns $1,243.71 a month.
   a. How much is this a year?

   b. How much is this a week?

33. **a.** Write 9 months as a number of years.

     b. Write 17 months as a number of years.

     c. Write 11.7 years as a number of months.

34. Lemons sell at $1.36 a dozen. You buy one lemon. How much are you charged?

35. At the post office, Mark bought different kinds of stamps. He bought thirty-two 15¢ stamps, fourteen 3¢ stamps, and fifty 9¢ stamps. How much did he spend there?

36. Midvale High School has 1.25 times as many students as Corbett High School has.
     a. Corbett High School has 1,580 students. How many students does Midvale High School have?

     b. Midvale High School has 1,580 students. How many students does Corbett High School have?

37.   Larry is 5.75 feet tall. Juanita is 5.5 feet tall. How many inches taller is Larry than Juanita?

38.   A water pipe has an outside diameter of 10 cm. The inside diameter is 9 cm. How thick is the pipe?

39.   A water pipe has an outside diameter of 12 cm. The pipe is .7 cm thick. What is the pipe's inside diameter?

40.   A water pipe has an inside diameter of 11 cm. The pipe is 1.2 cm thick. What is the pipe's outside diameter?

41. The Ralsons made up a budget. They decided to put aside part of each paycheck as follows:

     .25 for housing
     .2 for food and supplies
     .05 for medical expenses
     .11 for charities
     .17 for clothing
     .15 for miscellaneous
     .12 for savings

     What's wrong with this budget?

42. Garth typed an average of 47.2 words a minute for 11 minutes. How many words did he type in that time?

43. Ms. Bradley earns $7.25 an hour.
    a. How much does she earn for working 8 hours?

    b–c. She gets time and a half for overtime.
    b. How much does she get for 4 hours of overtime?

    c. She worked 54 hours one week, of which 14 hours were overtime. How much did she earn that week?

44. Big City's population was 1.8 million more than Midville's. Midville's population was 245,319. What was Big City's population?

45. Mrs. Thomas is 36.75 years old. Mr. Thomas is 34.25 years old. How many months older is Mrs. Thomas than Mr. Thomas?

46. What is the area of a room which is 12.5 feet wide and 14.25 feet long?

47. What is the area of a room which is 11 feet 6 inches wide and 13 feet 3 inches long?

48. Gasoline sells for $1.70 a gallon. How many gallons will $18.75 buy?

49. It took your car 15.8 gallons of gas to go 237 miles. What was the car's average gas mileage (in mpg)?

50. **a.** Write 15 minutes as a number of hours.

b. Write 80 minutes as a number of hours.

c. Write 2.75 hours as a number of minutes.

51. What is the average of 4.65, 3, 8.9, and 5.678?

52. A map uses a scale of 1.5 cm = 10 km. On this map, two cities are 5 cm apart. How many km apart are they really?

53. Roger earns an average of $28.35 a week on his paper route. How much is this a day?

54. Carolyn earns an average of $4.85 a day on her paper route. How much is this a week?

55. Mr. Walters bought 5 pounds of hamburger at $1.48 a pound. But .32 of the total weight cooked away as fat and water.
    a. How many pounds of the hamburger cooked away as fat and water?

    b. How many pounds of hamburger were left as meat?

    c. How much a pound did the meat cost Mr. Walters?

56. A circus sold 5,123 adults' tickets for $3.75 each. It also sold 7,526 children's tickets for $2.25 each. How much did the circus collect from these sales?

57. Light bulbs are on sale at 3 for $1.51. How much will you be charged if you buy just one of them?

58. The telephone charge for a call is 12.4¢ for the first minute plus 6.7¢ for each minute after that.

    a. How much is the charge for a 15-minute call?

    b. How much is the charge for a 22-minute call?

    c. The charge was $1.33. How long was the call?

59. Mr. Horner earns $10,751 a year.
    a. How much is this a week?

    b. How much is this a month?

60. **a.** Write 39 weeks as a number of years.

    b. Write 75 weeks as a number of years.

    c. Write 5.2 years as a number of weeks.

61. A car's average gas mileage is 11.8 mpg. At this rate, how far will it go on 17.3 gallons of gas?

62. The label on a can of beans shows the weight to be 484 grams or 1 pound 1 ounce. Based on this, how many grams are in an ounce?

63. Write these numbers in order from smallest to largest: .3, .12, .275, .0678, .2079

64. In baseball, a pitcher's earned run average (ERA) is figured as follows:
  • First, multiply 9 by the number of runs scored against him.
  • Then divide by the number of innings he pitched.
  • The result is rounded to 2 decimal places.

Find Ace's ERA in each of these cases:
  a. Ace pitched 4 innings in a game; 3 runs were scored against him.

  b. Ace pitched 6 innings in another game; 2 runs were scored against him.

  c. Ace pitched 12 innings in another game; 5 runs were scored against him.

  d. Ace pitched 2 innings in another game; no runs were scored against him.

65. Figure out Ace's overall ERA for the 4 games in problem 64 above.

66. A school carnival sold 758 tickets for 25¢ each, 2,315 tickets for 10¢ each, and 1,148 tickets for 5¢ each. How much money was collected?

67. What is the average of 5.6, 4.3, and 9.2?

68. A map uses a scale of 1.25 cm = 10 km. Two cities are really 127.8 km apart. How far apart will they be on the map?

69. Last year GIANT SUPERMARKET's sales were 1.7 times as much as the year before.
   a. The year before last sales were $4,565,267.50. How much were last year's sales?

   b. Last year sales were $5,536,716.57. How much were the sales for the year before last?

70. A store is having a sale. You can get .25 of the regular price off. A dryer usually sells there for $348.80. You buy it while it is on sale.

   a. How much discount do you get (in money)?

   b. What is the sale price of the dryer?

71. Corbett High School has 1,526 students, of which 1,015 are enrolled in music classes. So the ratio of students enrolled in music classes to those who are not is _____ to 1.

72. A jetliner travels 965 km in 2 hours. What is its average speed?

73. **a.** Write 5 days as a number of weeks.

   b. Write 17 days as a number of weeks

   c. Write 4.1 weeks as a number of days.

74. Radio station KVT is at 103.5 MHz. Radio station KVW is at 104.2 MHz. How many MHz is station KVT from station KVW?

75. Pat earned $5.80 baby-sitting, $27.40 on her paper route, and $13.85 doing odd jobs. She spent $9.78 on records, $11.65 on jeans, and $11.27 on sweaters.
    a. How much did she earn?

    b. How much did she spend?

    c. How much should she have left?

76. This year Gary will earn 2.5 times as much as he earned two years ago.
    a. Two years ago he earned $4,534.86. How much will he earn this year?

    b. This year he will earn $9,218.50. How much did he earn two years ago?

77.   A recipe to serve 4 people calls for 1.5 cups of flour. You decide to use the same recipe to serve a different number of people. How many cups of flour should you use if you make the recipe to serve

   a. 10 people?

   b. 35 people?

   c. 2 people?

   d. 3 people?

78.   The Gorans bought a refrigerator for $368.75. They paid $110.03 down. They paid the balance in 12 equal monthly payments.

   a. How much did they owe after the down payment?

   b. How much was each monthly payment?

79.   There are 24 cans of beans in a case of beans. The Warners can buy a case of beans for $6.95. If they buy the beans a can at a time, they must pay 31¢ each. How much will they save by buying a case of beans instead of buying them one can at a time?

80.   **a.**   Write 3 quarts as a number of gallons.

      b.   Write 17 quarts as a number of gallons.

      c.   Write 4.5 gallons as a number of quarts.

81.   To figure a grade point average in school, we do the following:
- First, we take the final grade from each course taken. We count 4 points for each A, 3 points for each B, 2 points for each C, 1 point for each D, and 0 points for each F.
- Next, we total all the points.
- Finally, we divide this answer by the number of grades. The final answer is rounded to 3 decimal places.

Figure out each student's grade point average.
  a.   Mary has earned 2 A's, 3 B's, 8 C's, 1 D.

  b.   John has earned 3 A's, 1 B, 9 C's, 3 D's, and 2 F's.

  c.   Bonnie has earned 10 A's and 5 B's.

  d.   Andrew has earned 5 A's and 10 B's.

82.   A water pipe has an outside diameter of 10.4 cm. The inside diameter is 7.6 cm. How thick is the pipe?

83. Big City's population is about 9.74 times as much as East City's population.

　　a. East City's population is 257,755. About how much is Big City's population?

　　b. Big City's population is 1,189.799. About how much is East City's population?

84. Cathy needs another $2,075 to cover her college expenses for the first year. She plans to work during the summer. She has been offered a job paying $4.65 an hour. (Write all answers to the nearest whole number.)

　　a. How many hours will she have to work in order to make the money she needs?

　　b. Cathy will work 8 hours a day. How many days will she have to work to make the needed money?

　　c. Cathy will work 7 hours each day. Each day she works, she will have to pay $1.25 for carfare, $2.25 for lunch, and 75¢ for rental of a uniform. How many days will she have to work to make the money she needs for college?

　　d. Cathy will work 8 hours each day. Besides the expenses listed in question c above, the payroll office will withhold $9.67 each day for various taxes. How many days will Cathy have to work to make the money she needs for college?

85. A car travels 3 miles in 30 minutes. What is its average speed (in mph)?

86.   A jetliner averaged 327.6 mph for 3 hours and 21 minutes. How far did it go in this time?

87.   A map uses a scale of 1.25 cm = 10 km. On this map, two cities are 6.8 cm apart. How many km are they really apart?

88.   A large washer has an outside diameter of 11.76 cm. The washer is 1.23 cm wide. What is the washer's inside diameter?

89.   The Bartons bought a car for $6,268.35. They traded in their old car for $2,500. They agreed to pay the balance in 36 equal monthly payments. The interest charge for financing the balance was $796.45.

   a.   What was the balance after the trade-in allowance?

   b.   What was the balance after the interest charge was added?

   c.   How much was each monthly payment?

90. In Corbett High School, the ratio of students who take math classes to students who do not take math classes is 1.3 to 1. Corbett High School has 1,472 students.

    a. How many do not take math classes?

    b. How many take math classes?

91. What is the average of 3.2 and 4.68?

92.   **a.** Write 4 hours 25 minutes as a number of hours.

    b. Write 39 weeks 6 days as a number of weeks.

    c. Write 39 weeks 6 days as a number of years. (Use 365 days in a year.)

93. Nancy had the following test scores: 68, 100, 80, 92, and 91.

    a. What was her average score for these tests?

  b–c. The teacher rounds the average to the nearest whole number.

    b. What average will the teacher show?

    c. Suppose the teacher drops the lowest score when computing the average. Now what average will the teacher show?

94. A piece of drawing paper is 46 cm long and 30 cm wide. A border of 2.5 cm must be left all the way around it. The part of the paper which can be used for the drawing is _____cm long and _____cm wide.

95. A jetliner travels 480 km in 36 minutes. What is its average speed (in kph)?

96. Mr. Nestor bought 5.34 pounds of meat at $1.36 a pound. How much was he charged?

97. There are about 28.35 grams in an ounce.
   a. About how many grams are in 5 ounces?

   b. About how many grams are in one pound?

   c. About how many ounces are in 80 grams?

   d. About how many pounds are in 5,286 grams?

98. Ms. Wheeler is a salesperson. She earns a salary of $89.50 a week. She also gets a commission of 4¢ on each dollar she takes in for goods sold. Last week her sales totaled $3,469.25. How much did she earn last week?

99. A parking lot charges $2 for the first half-hour and 75¢ an hour (or part of an hour) after that. Figure out the parking charge for each of the following.
     a. Ms. Aston parked her car there $3\frac{1}{2}$ hours.

     b. Mr. Uhler parked his car there $2\frac{3}{4}$ hours.

     c. Ms. Capra parked her car there $4\frac{2}{3}$ hours.

     d. Mr. Farmer parked his car there 45 minutes.

     e. Ms. Grebin parked her car there from 8:45 A.M. to 11:25 A.M.

100. In problem 99 above, the charge for Ms. Rogers' car was $7.25. For how long was she charged?

101. The Orlands bought furniture for $1,525.36. They paid $210.15 down. The balance was to be paid in 12 equal monthly payments. The store added a finance charge of $159.83.

   a. How much did they owe after the down payment?

   b. How much did they owe after the finance charge was added?

   c. How much was each monthly payment?

102. **a.** Write 45 centimeters as a number of meters.

   b. Write 267 centimeters as a number of meters.

   c. Write 1.87 meters as a number of centimeters.

103. It took Mandy 2.3 hours to do a homework assignment. It took her brother 1.7 hours to do the same assignment. How many minutes longer did it take Mandy than it took her brother to do the assignment?

104. The ratio of acid to water in a solution is 3.25 to 1.
   a. How much acid should be used to make 17 liters of the solution?

   b. The chemist used 5 ml of water for the solution. How much acid should he use?

   c. The chemist used 5 ml of acid for the solution. How much water should he use?

105. You buy 24.3 liters of gasoline at 45.5¢ a liter. You also buy 2 liters of oil at 98¢ a liter.
   a. What is your total bill?

   b. You pay with a $20 bill. How much change do you get?

106. A moving company charges 15¢ a pound plus 50¢ a mile. Their minimum charge is $75. Figure out how much it cost each person to move.
   a. Ms. Verind had the company move things weighing 1,500 pounds a distance of 25 miles.

   b. Mr. Inness had the company move things weighing 3,523 pounds a distance of 500 miles.

   c. Ms. Akers had the company move something weighing 300 pounds a distance of 10 miles.

107. There are 2.54 centimeters in an inch.
    a. How many centimeters are in 12 inches?

    b. How many centimeters are in a yard?

    c. How many inches are in one centimeter?

    d. How many inches are in 3 centimeters?

108. Peter bought 3.67 pounds of cheese at $1.38 a pound. How much did he pay for it?

109. Greg's test scores were 89, 70, 80, 100, and 95. The second test counted as double weight. The fourth test counted as triple weight.
    a. How many test grades will the teacher count when averaging Greg's test scores?

    b. What was Greg's average test score?

    c. Suppose the teacher drops the lowest test score. To the nearest whole number, what will Greg's average be?

Decimals

Math Word Problems Level B

110. On the inside, a closed box is 15 inches high, 18 inches wide, and 27 inches long.
  a. What are its measurements in feet?

  b. How many cubic feet of air does it hold?

111. There are about 1.6 km in a mile.
  a. About how many km are in 30 miles?

  b. About how many km are in 55 miles?

  c. A speed of 50 mph is about the same as a speed of _____ kph.

  d. About how many miles are there in one km?

  e. About how many miles are there in 100 km?

  f. A speed of 50 kph is about the same as a speed of _____ mph.

112. What is the exact area of a rectangle 1.3 cm wide and 2.58 cm long?

113.   One side of a square measures 1.25 inches. What is the exact area of the square?

114.   **a.**   Write 75 meters as a number of kilometers.

   b.   Write 1,776 meters as a number of kilometers.

   c.   Write 3.25 kilometers as a number of meters.

115.   Gasoline sells for 93.8¢ a half-gallon. You buy 7.5 gallons. You give the attendant $20. How much change do you get?

116.   A piece of tubing has an inside diameter of 11.37 cm. The tubing is 1.48 cm thick. What is the tubing's outside diameter?

117.   The gas tank of your car holds 80 liters. Yesterday it took 57.3 liters to fill the tank. How much was in the tank just before it was filled?

118. A toolmaker measured a part four times. These were the measurements he found: 2.5986 cm, 2.6124 cm, 2.5775 cm, 2.5943 cm. What was the average measurement?

119. A group of eight people bought five pizzas at $4.80 for each pizza. They split the cost equally among themselves. How much did each person pay?

120. A map uses a scale of 1.4 cm = 17 km. On this map, two cities are 11.9 cm apart. How many km are the cities really apart?

121. A map uses a scale of 1.4 cm = 17 km. Two cities are really 123.25 km apart. How far apart are they on the map?

122. A car travels 400 km in 4 hours 39 minutes. What is its average speed (in kph)?

123.   A car averaged 45.6 mph for 5 hours 18 minutes. How far did it go in this time?

124.   There are about 3.785 liters in a gallon.

      a. About how many liters are in 3 gallons?

      b. About how many liters are in 4.6 gallons?

      c. About how many gallons are in a liter?

      d. About how many gallons are in 5 liters?

      e. About how many quarts are in a liter?

      f. About how many quarts are in 4 liters?

      g. Is a liter more than or less than a quart?

125.   Harlow ran a mile in 4 minutes. What was his speed in mph?

126.   The gas tank of your car holds 21 gallons. You fill it up. You drive 189 miles and fill it up again. This time it takes 15 gallons to fill the tank. What was your car's average gas mileage (in mpg)?

127.   To figure out his selling price, a store owner multiplies his cost by 1.25.
   a. For how much will he sell something which cost him $97.60?

   b. He will sell something for $145.25. How much did it cost him?

3. Percents 1

INSTRUCTIONS

A. No information is missing. No problem is meant to trick you.

Example

Problem: Jacobs earned $20,000 last year. This year he got a 20% raise. How much will his income be this year?

Answer: $24,000 (Assume he had no other income. Assume he worked all year both years. Assume he was paid what he earned last year. Assume he will be paid this year's salary this year.)

B. In general, if a percent is not a whole number, write the remainder as a fraction, not as a decimal.

Example

Problem: Rawlins earned $20,000 last year. This year she will earn $24,000. What percent of this year's earnings were last year's earnings?

Answer: $83\frac{1}{3}$ % (not 83.3% or 83.33% or 83.333%, etc.)

1. Dalton is a salesman. He gets a commission of 8% on all the sales he makes. His sales last week were $3,420. How much was his commission?

2. Dalton is a salesman. He gets a commission of 8% on all the sales he makes. His commission last week was $345.20. How much were his sales last week?

3. Dalton is a salesman. He gets a commission on all the sales he makes. His sales last week were $4,400. His commission on these sales was $308. What percent of the sales was his commission?

4. Daniels paid 20% down on a $6,000 car. How much did he pay down?

5. Daniels paid $6,000 as a 20 % down payment on a boat. How much was the boat?

6. Daniels paid $6,000 down on a $40,000 house. What percent of the price of the house was the down payment?

7. North is a saleswoman. She gets a weekly salary of $100. She also gets a commission on 6% on all the sales she makes. Her sales last week were $3,420. How much did she earn last week?

8. North is a saleswoman. She gets a weekly salary of $100. She also gets a commission of 6% on all the sales she makes. She earned $347.20 last week. How much were her sales last week?

9. North is a saleswoman. She gets a weekly salary of $100. She also gets a commission on all the sales she makes. She earned $323.20 last week. Her sales last week were $5,580. What percent of the sales was her commission?

10. A bank pays 8% annual interest on a savings certificate.
    a. What monthly rate of interest does it pay?

    b. What quarterly rate of interest does it pay?

11. A bank pays 7% annual interest on a savings certificate. Smith buys a $4,000 certificate. How much interest does he get on this each year?

12. Smith invested $5,000 in a savings certificate. He gets $450 a year in interest on the certificate. What yearly interest rate does the certificate pay?

13. Smith put some money in a savings certificate which earns 8% a year. The yearly interest is $600. How much did Smith invest?

14.   Marge's score on a test was 85%. She had 34 problems right.
    a.   How many problems were on the test?

    b.   What percent of the problems on the test did Marge get wrong?

    c.   How many problems did Marge get wrong?

15.   Marge took a test with 40 problems on it. She got 36 right.
    a.   What was Marge's score on the test?

    b.   What percent of the number of problems on the test did Marge get right?

    c.   How many problems did Marge get wrong?

    d.   What percent of the number of problems on the test did Marge get wrong?

16.   Marge's score on a test was 84%. The test had 25 problems on it.
   a. What percent of the problems did Marge get wrong?

   b. How many problems did Marge get right?

   c. How many problems did Marge get wrong?

   d. What percent of the number of problems wrong was the number of problems on the test?

   e. What percent of the number of problems wrong was the number of problems right?

   f. What percent of the number of problems on the test was the number of problems Marge got wrong?

17.   A dealer offers to sell you a car listed at $7,000 for $6,860.
   a.   How much discount is the dealer offering?

   b.   What percent discount is the dealer offering?

   c.   What percent of the list price is the price the dealer quotes you?

18.   A dealer offers to sell you a car at 3% off the list price. He quotes you a price of $6,596.
   a.   The price quoted you is what percent of the list price?

   b.   How much is the list price?

   c.   The list price is what percent of the price quoted you?

   d.   How much money is the discount offered you?

57

19. At two different dealers, you price a new car which has a list price of $7,500. One dealer offers you a 3% discount. The other offers you a 2% discount.

   a. How much money is the first dealer's offered discount?

   b. How much money is the second dealer's offered discount?

   c. How much money would you save by buying the car at the first dealer's place?

   d. What is the percent difference in discounts offered? Take this percent of the list price. Is the answer the same as your "c" answer?

   e. If you buy from the first dealer, what percent of the list price do you pay?

   f. How much do you pay if you buy the car from the first dealer?

   g. If you buy from the second dealer, what percent of the list price do you pay?

   h. How much do you pay if you buy the car from the second dealer?

   i. Subtract your "f" answer from your "h" answer. Is the result the same as your "c" answer?

20.   **a.**   What percent is $\frac{3}{4}$?

      b.   What percent is $\frac{1}{4}$?

21.   **a.**   Write 20% as a fraction.

      b.   Write 80% as a fraction.

22.   Bradley's car was getting 20 mpg. She had it tuned up. Now it gets 25 mph.
      a.   What percent of the new gas mileage was the old gas mileage?

      b.   What percent of the old gas mileage is the new gas mileage?

      c.   What percent of the new gas mileage is the improvement in gas mileage?

      d.   What percent of the old gas mileage is the improvement in gas mileage?

23. Bradley's car was getting poor mileage. She had it tuned up. Now it gets 20 mpg. This is a 25% improvement over the old gas mileage.

    a. What percent of the old gas mileage is the new gas mileage?

    b. What was the old gas mileage?

    c. What percent of the new gas mileage was the old gas mileage?

    d. What percent of the new gas mileage is the improvement in the gas mileage?

24. **a.** Write $\frac{1}{10}$ as a percent.

    b. Write $\frac{2}{10}$ as a percent.

    c. Write $\frac{3}{10}$ as a percent.

    d. Write $\frac{4}{10}$ as a percent.

    e. Write $\frac{5}{10}$ as a percent.

    f. Write $\frac{9}{10}$ as a percent.

25.   Bradley's car was getting 20 mpg. She had it tuned up. Now the gas mileage is 20% better than it was before.

    a.   What percent of the old gas mileage is the new gas mileage?

    b.   What is the new gas mileage?

    c.   What percent of the new gas mileage was the old gas mileage?

    d.   What percent of the old gas mileage was the improvement in gas mileage?

26.   You buy a new car. The unpaid balance is $4,000. You arrange to finance the car for two years. The finance charge is figured on the unpaid balance. The charge is $720.

    a.   What is the finance charge for one year?

    b.   What percent of the unpaid balance is the yearly finance charge?

    c.   What percent of the unpaid balance is the total finance charge?

27. **a.** Write $\frac{1}{1}$ as a percent.

  b. Write $\frac{2}{2}$ as a percent.

  c. Write $\frac{3}{3}$ as a percent.

  d. Write $\frac{4}{4}$ as a percent.

  e. Write $\frac{10}{10}$ as a percent.

  f. Write $\frac{389}{389} \times \frac{247}{247}$ as a percent.

28. You buy a new car. The unpaid balance is $5,000. You arrange to finance the car for two years. The finance charge is figured on the unpaid balance. The charge is $1,100.
  a. What percent of the unpaid balance is the finance charge?

  b. What percent of the unpaid balance is the yearly finance charge?

29. The yearly finance charge on a new car is 8% of the original unpaid balance. You buy a new car. After the down payment, you still owe $5,000. How much is the finance charge for

  a. one year?

  b. two years?

  c. three years?

  d. four years?

  e. six months?

  f. eighteen months?

  g. thirty months?

  h. forty-two months?

30. The yearly finance charge on a new car is 8% of the original unpaid balance. You buy a new car. The finance charge for three years is $1,560.
    a. What is the finance charge for one year?

    b. What was the original unpaid balance on the car?

31. You buy a used car. The unpaid balance is $2,000. You arrange to finance the car for three years. The finance charge is figured on the unpaid balance. The charge is $720. What percent of the unpaid balance is the yearly finance charge?

32. Midstate levies a sales tax on all retail sales. Big Store's retail sales, including the tax, were $2,201.80. The retail sales, not including the tax, were $2,137.67.
    a. How much tax was collected?

    b. What percent of the sales, not including the tax, were the sales including the tax?

    c. What percent is the Midstate sales tax on retail sales?

33.   Midstate levies a 4% sales tax on all retail sales. Big Store's retail sales, including the tax, were $4,616.04.

    a.   How much were Big Store's retail sales, not including the tax?

    b.   How much tax does Big Store owe Midstate?

34.   Midstate levies a 4% sales tax on all retail sales. Big Store's retail sales, not including the tax, were $4,616.04. How much sales tax does Big Store owe Midstate?

35.   Crawford made $10,000 last year. She will make $15,000 this year.

    a.   What percent of this year's earnings were last year's earnings?

    b.   What percent of last year's earnings are this year's earnings?

    c.   By what percent did last year's earnings increase?

36. Crawford made $10,000 last year. She got a 25% raise this year.

    a. What percent of last year's earnings are this year's earnings?

    b. How much is she making this year?

    c. What percent of this year's earnings are last year's earnings?

37. Crawford is making $21,000 this year. This is a 12% improvement over her salary last year.

    a. What percent of last year's salary is this year's salary?

    b. How much did Crawford make last year?

    c. What percent of this year's salary was last year's salary?

38. Garner is a machinist. She used to make 50 parts an hour. Now, she makes 112% as many parts per hour as she used to make. How many parts per hour does she make?

39. Garner is a machinist. She used to make 50 parts an hour. Now, she makes 112% more parts per hour than she used to make. How many parts per hour does she make?

40. Garner is a machinist. She used to make 50 parts an hour. Now, she has improved this production by 10%.

    a. What percent of the old hourly number of parts is the new hourly number of parts?

    b. How many parts does she now make each hour?

41. Garner is a machinist. She makes 66 parts an hour. This is a 10% improvement over the number of parts per hour she used to make.

    a. What percent of the old hourly number of parts is the new hourly number of parts?

    b. How many parts did she used to make each hour?

    c. What percent of the new hourly number of parts was the old hourly number of parts?

42. Garner is a machinist. She used to make 40 parts an hour. Now, she makes 50 parts an hour.

    a. What percent of the old hourly number of parts is the new hourly number of parts?

    b. What percent of the old hourly number of parts is the improvement in production?

    c. What percent of the new hourly number of parts is the old hourly number of parts?

43. A publisher sells books to dealers for 25% less than the list price. The price of a book sold to a dealer is $15.

    a. What percent of the list price is the price to the dealer?

    b. How much is the list price of the book?

    c. What percent of the $15 price does the dealer pay?

    d. What percent of the $15 price is the list price?

    e. What percent of the price charged the dealer is the list price?

    f. What percent of the list price does the dealer pay?

44. **a.** Write 150% as a fraction.

   b. Write 50% as a fraction.

45. A publisher sells books to dealers for 25% less than the list price. The list price of a book is $15.
   a. How much discount on this book would a dealer get?

   b. What price would a dealer pay?

   c. What percent of the list price would a dealer pay?

   d. What percent of the price charged the dealer is the list price?

46. A publisher charges a dealer $6.60 for a book which has a list price of $11.
   a. What percent of the list price is the price charged the dealer?

   b. What percent of the list price is the dealer's discount?

   c. What percent of the list price is $4.40?

   d. What percent of the price charged the dealer is the list price?

47. **a.** Write $\frac{3}{4}$ as a percent.

b. Write $\frac{6}{8}$ as a percent.

c. Write $\frac{9}{12}$ as a percent.

d. Write $\frac{12}{16}$ as a percent.

e. Write $\frac{30}{40}$ as a percent.

f. Write $\frac{75}{100}$ as a percent.

48. A piece of metal is .2 cm thick. Jason measured it as .17 cm.
a. What percent of the real thickness was the measured thickness?

b. What percent of the measured thickness is the real thickness?

c. What percent of the real thickness was the amount of error in the measured thickness?

49. Jason measured the thickness of a piece of metal as .02 cm. The metal was really .2 cm thick.

    a. What percent of the measured thickness was the real thickness?

    b. What percent of the real thickness was the measured thickness?

    c. By what percent of the real thickness was the measured thickness in error?

50. A piece of metal is .2 cm thick. Jason measured it as 10% thinner than it was. What was Jason's measurement of the metal?

51. A piece of metal is .2 cm thick. Jason measured it as 10% thicker than it was. What was Jason's measurement of the metal?

52. Edwards bought a TV set on sale for $300. Its usual price was $375.

    a. What percent of the usual price was the sale price?

    b. What percent of the usual price did Edwards save by buying the TV set on sale?

53. Edwards bought a $500 TV set on sale at a 15% discount.
   a. How much was the discount?

   b. How much did she pay for the TV set?

   c. What percent of the usual price was the sale price?

   d. How much did Edwards save by buying the TV set while it was on sale?

54. Edwards paid $387 for a TV set which was on sale at a 14% discount.
   a. What per cent of the usual price was the sale price?

   b. What was the usual price of the TV set?

   c. What percent of the sale price was the usual price?

55. You clip a coupon from the newspaper which gives you 25¢ off the regular price of a package of dog food. The dog food usually costs 75¢. What percent of the regular price do you save by using the coupon?

56. You clip a coupon from the newspaper which offers you a $1 refund from the manufacturer if you mail it to them with a label from their product. You buy the product for $3.23 plus 4% sales tax. You mail the coupon and label to the manufacturer at a cost of 15¢ for the stamp and 1¢ for the envelope. The manufacturer sends you a check for $1.

   a. How much did it cost you to send the coupon to the manufacturer?

   b. How much profit did you make from sending the coupon to the manufacturer?

   c. How much sales tax did you pay on the product?

   d. How much (total) did you pay for the product at the store?

   e. What percent of the total you paid was your profit?

   f. How much did the product end up costing you?

   g. What percent of the original sale price (including tax) was your actual cost of the product?

57. **a.** Write 95% as a fraction.

b. Write 5% as a fraction.

58. Woods gets a hit 25% of the times she bats. She has 38 hits.
   a. How many times has she batted?

b. How many times at bat has she failed to get a hit?

59. Three out of every four times at bat, Woods fails to get a hit.
   a. What percent of her times at bat does Woods not get a hit?

b. What percent of her times at bat does Woods get a hit?

60. Woods got 57 hits out of 190 times at bat.
   a. What percent of the times at bat did Woods get a hit?

b. What percent of the times at bat did Woods not get a hit?

61.   Woods gets a hit 32% of the times she bats. She has batted 150 times.
   a. How many hits did she get?

   b. How many times at bat did she not get a hit?

62.   Borton sued Jones. Borton's attorney charged 30% of the amount the court made
   Jones pay Borton. The court made Jones pay Borton $50,000.
   a. How much did the attorney get?

   b. How much did Borton have left?

   c. What percent of the awarded amount did Borton have left?

   d. What percent of the awarded amount did the attorney get?

   e. The amount of money Borton paid the attorney was what percent of the amount
        Borton got to keep?

63.   Borton sued Jones. Borton's attorney charged 30% of the amount the court made Jones pay Borton. After Borton paid the attorney, Borton had $42,000 left.

     a.   What percent of the awarded amount did Borton have left?

     b.   What was the awarded amount?

     c.   What percent of the amount Borton had left was the awarded amount?

     d.   How much did the attorney get?

64.   **a.**   Write $\frac{1}{5}$ as a percent.

     b.   Write $\frac{2}{5}$ as a percent.

     c.   Write $\frac{3}{5}$ as a percent.

     d.   Write $\frac{4}{5}$ as a percent.

65. A TV station charges 50% more for running an ad during prime time than for running the same ad in the afternoon. An ad costs $3,375 during prime time.
   a. What percent of the charges for an afternoon ad is the charge for a prime time ad?

   b. How much does the $3,375 prime time ad cost as an afternoon ad?

66. A TV station charges 50% more for running an ad during prime time than for running the same ad in the afternoon. An ad costs $2,700 in the afternoon. What is the cost of running the same ad during prime time?

67. At a certain TV station, an ad which costs $1,900 in the afternoon costs $2,660 during prime time.
   a. What percent of the afternoon cost is the prime time cost?

   b. What is the difference (in money) between the two costs?

   c. What percent of the afternoon cost is the difference in costs?

   d. What percent of the prime time cost is the afternoon cost?

68. **a.** Write 225% as a fraction.

b. Write 125% as a fraction.

c. Write 25% as a fraction.

69. Andrews bought a ring for $10 off the usual $40 price.
   a. What percent discount did she get?

b. What percent of the usual price did she pay?

c. How much was the discount (in money)?

d. How much did she pay (in money)?

70.   Andrews bought a ring for $10 off the usual price. She paid $30 for it.
       a.   What was the usual price of the ring?

       b.   What percent off the regular price did Andrews get?

       c.   What percent of the usual price did Andrews pay?

       d.   What percent of the regular price was the discounted price?

       e.   What percent of the discounted price was the regular price?

71.   Andrews bought a $40 ring at a 30% discount.
       a.   How much was the discount?

       b.   How much did Andrews pay for the ring?

       c.   What percent of the regular price did Andrews pay?

       d.   What percent of the price Andrews paid was the regular price?

72.   Al takes $40% longer to do a job than you take. The job takes you 20 minutes.
       a.   How long does the job take Al?

       b.   What percent of the time the job takes you to do does the job take Al to do?

       c.   What percent of the time the job takes Al to do does the job take you to do?

73.   Al takes 63 minutes to do a job which takes you only 45 minutes.
       a.   What percent of the time the job takes you to do does the job take Al to do?

       b.   How much longer (in minutes) does the job take Al than it takes you?

       c.   As a percent, how much longer does the job take Al than it takes you?

74.   Al takes 40% longer to do a job than you take. Al takes 49 minutes to do the job.
       a.   What percent of the time you take for the job does Al take?

       b.   How much time do you take for the job?

       c.   How many minutes longer than you take does Al take for the job?

       d.   What percent of the time the job takes you is the extra time the job takes Al?

75.   For Werner's car, the air pressure in the tires is supposed to be 24 psi. The air pressure is really 30 psi.

   a.   What percent of the ideal air pressure is the real air pressure?

   b.   By what percent are the tires overinflated?

   c.   What percent of the real air pressure is the ideal air pressure?

76.   For Werner's car, the air pressure in the tires is supposed to be 25 psi. The tires are underinflated by 20%

   a.   What percent of the ideal air pressure is the real air pressure?

   b.   What is the air pressure in the tires?

77.   On Werner's car, the air pressure in the tires is 26 psi. This is 4% higher than the ideal air pressure.

   a.   What percent of the ideal air pressure is the real air pressure?

   b.   What is the ideal air pressure?

78. **a.** Write 1800% as a fraction.

     b. Write 180% as a fraction.

     c. Write 18% as a fraction.

     d. Write 1.8% as a fraction.

79. This year a house is worth $50,000. Last year it was worth $40,000.
     a. What percent of last year's value is this year's value of the house?

     b. In money, what is the difference in the two values of the house?

     c. What percent of last year's value is the difference in the two values?

     d. What percent of this year's value is last year's value of the house?

80.   This year a house is worth 10% more than it was worth last year. Last year the house was worth $44,000.

   a.   In money, how much more is the house worth this year?

   b.   How much is the house worth this year?

   c.   What percent of last year's value is this year's value of the house?

   d.   What percent of this year's value was last year's value of the house?

81.   **a.**   Write 7000% as a fraction.

   b.   Write 700% as a fraction.

   c.   Write 70% as a fraction.

   d.   Write 7% as a fraction.

   e.   Write .7% as a fraction.

82.   This year a house is worth 10% more than it was worth last year. This year the house
      is worth $44,000.
      a. What percent of last year's value is this year's value of the house?

      b. How much was the house worth last year?

      c. What is the difference between this year's value and last year's value of the house?

      d. What percent of last year's value is the difference in values?

83.   Loring's dental insurance pays 60% of the cost of dentures. Loring had dental plates
      made which cost a total of $950.
      a. How much of the cost did the insurance company pay?

      b. What percent of the cost did Loring pay?

      c. How much did Loring pay?

84. Loring's dental insurance pays 60% of the cost of dentures. Loring paid $344 for dentures.

   a. What percent of the total cost did Loring pay?

   b. What was the total cost of the dentures?

   c. How much of the cost did the insurance company pay?

85. Big Store offers a 20% discount on all purchases after the first $20 total. At Big Store, you buy goods totaling $30 (before the discount).

   a. On how much of the total do you get a discount?

   b. How much is the discount?

   c. How much do you pay?

86. Big Store offers a 20% discount on all purchases after the first $20 total. You buy goods there and pay them $60.
   a. How much of the amount you paid was for goods bought at the regular price?

   b. How much of the amount you paid was for goods bought at the discounted price?

   c. On goods you bought at a discounted price, what percent of the regular price did you pay?

   d. What was the regular price of the goods you bought at a discount?

   e. What was the regular price of all the goods you bought?

87.   **a.**   Write $\frac{2}{1}$ as a percent.

b.   Write $\frac{3}{1}$ as a percent.

c.   Write $\frac{4}{1}$ as a percent.

d.   Write 5 as a percent.

e.   Write 11 as a percent.

f.   Write 251 as percent.

g.   Write 3897 as a percent.

88.   A thrift shop sells clothes for 75% less than the usual price. Ms. Harper bought a dress there for $6.
    a.   What percent of the usual price did Ms. Harper pay?

b.   What was the usual price of the dress?

c.   How much did Ms. Harper save?

89. A thrift shop sells clothes for 75% less than the usual price. At the thrift shop, Ms. Harper bought a dress whose usual price was $20.
  a. How much did she pay for the dress?

  b. How much did she save by buying the dress at the thrift shop?

  c. What percent of the usual price did she save by buying the dress at the thrift shop?

90. Ms. Harper bought a dress at a thrift shop for $5. The usual price of the dress was $12.50.
  a. What percent of the usual price did Ms. Harper pay?

  b. What percent of the usual price was the discount Ms. Harper got from the thrift shop?

  c. How much did Ms. Harper save by buying the dress at the thrift shop?

91. The local drug store offers a 50% discount on medicines sold to senior citizens. Mr. Gorman, a senior citizen, bought medicine for $2.50 there.
   a. What percent of the usual price did Mr. Gorman pay?

   b. What is the usual price of the medicine he bought?

   c. What percent of the price paid by Mr. Gorman is the usual price of the medicine?

92. The local drug store offers a 50% discount on medicines sold to senior citizens. Mr. Gorman, a senior citizen, bought medicine there which had a regular price of $8.60. How much did Mr. Gorman pay for the medicine?

93. The local drug store offers a discount on medicines sold to senior citizens. Mr. Gorman, a senior citizen, bought medicine there for $5.40. The usual price of the medicine was $9.
   a. How much less than the usual price did Mr. Gorman pay?

   b. What percent of the usual price did Mr. Gorman pay?

   c. What percent of the usual price was the discount given Mr. Gorman?

4. Percents 2

INSTRUCTIONS

A. No problem is meant to trick you.

Example

Problem: A store advertises a 20% discount on all books. The regular price of one book is $5. What is the sale price?

Answer: $4 (Assume the book is in the store mentioned. Assume the advertising was truthful. Assume the store did not normally give a 20% discount on books.)

B. No information is missing.

Example

Problem: A jacket usually sells for $40. You buy it at 15% off. How much do you spend?

Answer: $34 (Assume you don't buy anything else. Assume you pay the right amount. Assume there is no sales tax.)

C. If a percent answer does not come out to a whole number, write it as a mixed number, not as a decimal.

Example

Problem: What percent of 80 is 70?

Answer: $87\frac{1}{2}$ % (not 87.5%)

1. Angel's age is 75% of Heather's age. Heather is 8 years old. How old is Angel?

2. What percent of one minute is
    a. 30 seconds?

    b. 45 seconds?

    c. 50 seconds?

3. Of the field goals attempted, the Rams have succeeded 13 times. They have been unsuccessful 7 times. What percent of the time have they been
    a. successful?

    b. unsuccessful?

4. A newspaper interviewed 780 people last week. Of these people, 95% knew that George Washington was the first president of the United States.
    a. How many people knew who the first president of the United States was?

    b. How many people did not know who the first president of the United States was?

5. A left fielder has made errors 5.1% of the time. What percent of the time has she not made errors?

6. A car manufacturer says it will increase the prices of its new cars by 4%. One of its cars now sells for $6,240. What will the price be when the increase takes effect?

7. A loan shark makes loans at an interest rate of 10% a week. The interest is on any amount you owe him, including interest. You borrow $100 from him. How much do you owe him at the end of
  a. one week?

  b. two weeks if you don't pay anything before that?

  c. three weeks if you don't pay anything before that?

  d. four weeks if you don't pay anything before that?

  e. two weeks if you paid $30 at the end of the first week?

  f. three weeks if you paid $40 at the end of the first week and $50 at the end of the second week?

8. Mr. Ingle earned $370 last week. Of this, 6.14% was withheld for social security tax. How much was withheld for this tax?

9. A pound is what percent of
   a. 8 ounces?

   b. 24 ounces?

   c. 32 ounces?

10. Last year Mr. James made $14,850.
   a. This year he got a 12% raise. How much is he making this year?

   b. This year he got a raise and is making $16,038. What percent was his raise?

11. You bought some stock a year ago for $1,200. How much is it worth now if its value
     a. has increased 10%?

     b. has decreased 10%?

     c. has increased 5%?

     d. has increased $\frac{1}{2}$%?

     e. has decreased .3%?

     f. has increased 50%?

12. The Lions have made field goals 60% of the times they attempted them. They have
     attempted 15 field goals. How many times have their attempts been unsuccessful?

13. Ms. Fraser's salary is $450 a week. A percent of the $450 is withheld for income tax. How much is withheld if the payroll office withholds
     a. 14%?

     b. 19%?

     c. 22.2%?

14. You bought a new car a year ago for $6,340. It is worth 23% less now.
     a. How much has it decreased in value?

     b. How much is it still worth?

15. A store advertises, "$\frac{1}{3}$ off the regular price for everything inside!"
     a. What percent discount are they offering?

     b. What percent of the regular price is the sale price?

16. An ice hockey goalie has a "saves" record of 71.2%. What percent of the time did his opponents succeed when they tried to score against him?

17.   A salesperson works on a commission basis. She gets 3% of all the sales she makes. How much did she make last week if her sales were
  a. $100?

  b. $10,000?

  c. $85,250?

18.   Last week the salesperson from problem 17 above made $438.72. How much were her sales?

19.   The Comptons were injured in an accident which was not their fault. An attorney said her charge for taking the case to court would be 30% of whatever the Comptons were awarded.
  a. Suppose the Comptons were awarded $40,000. How much did the attorney get?

  b. Suppose the Comptons lost the case and were not awarded anything. How much did the attorney get?

20. The Tigers won 20 games, tied 2 games, and lost 18 games. What percent of the
     games did they
     a. win?

     b. tie?

     c. lose?

21. You bought some stock a year ago for $2,500. By what percent has the value in-
     creased if the stock is now worth
     a. $3,000?

     b. $2,600?

     c. $2,550?

     d. $5,000?

22.   What percent of a foot is
      a. 1 inch?

      b. 3 inches?

      c. 8 inches?

23.   Handy Suppliers offers a 3% discount if the customer pays within 10 days. You bought supplies totaling $548.30 from them. How much will you save if you pay them within 10 days?

24.   Groceries now cost 12% more than they did last year.
      a. Last year food cost the Athertons $45 a week. How much does that same kind of food cost this year?

      b. This year the Bortons are spending $77 a week for food. How much did the same kind of food cost last year?

25.   Martin earns $12,000 a year; Nelson earns $15,000 a year.
      a. By what percent are Nelson's earnings more than Martin's?

      b. By what percent are Martin's earnings less than Nelson's?

26. You have a new job. At the end of each of the first three years, you will get a 10% raise. You will not get other raises in this time. Your starting salary is $12,000 a year.
    a–c. How much is your yearly raise at the end of
    a. the first year?

    b. the second year?

    c. the third year?

    d. How much is your yearly salary at the start of the fourth year?

27. You buy a new car for $5,700. You pay $2,200 down. You finance the rest for 3 years. The yearly interest is 8% of the original unpaid balance.
    a. How much is the interest charge for a year?

    b. How much is the interest charge you must pay?

28. Two years ago typing paper sold for $6 a ream. Now it is $10.50 a ream. By what percent did the price increase?

29. Of the students in the Corbett School District, 40% ride the bus to school.
   a. The district has 6,150 students. How many ride the bus to school?

   b. How many students does the district have if 3,296 students ride the bus to school?

   c. If 5,115 students do not ride the bus to school, how many students does the district have?

30. Shoes are on sale at 25% off. How much does a pair of shoes
   a. sell for now if the regular price is $12.60?

   b. usually sell for if the sale price is $12.60?

31. A dryer costs 11% more this year than last year.
   a. Last year the dryer cost $220. How much is it this year?

   b. This year the dryer costs $349.65. How much was it last year?

32. It is customary to leave a 15% tip for good service in a restaurant. What is the usual tip for good service if the bill totals
    a. $8?

    b. $9.60?

    c. $25?

33. Large candy bars are on sale at $33\frac{1}{3}$ % off. How much does a candy bar
    a. cost on sale if its regular price is $1.50?

    b. usually cost if its sale price is 90¢

34. Of the students in the vocal music class, 70% took the class last year, too.
    a. The class had 80 students. How many did not take the class last year?

    b. There are 33 students who did not take the class last year. How many are in the class?

35. What percent of one gallon is
    a. 1 quart?

    b. 4 quarts?

    c. 10 quarts?

36. Last week a container of milk sold for 65¢. Now it is 70¢.
    a. What percent of last week's price is this week's price?

    b. By what percent did the price increase?

    c. What percent of this week's price was last week's price?

    d. By what percent was last week's price lower?

37. Mr. Garner's weekly salary is $400. A percent of the $400 is withheld for income tax. What percent was withheld if the amount withheld was

   a. $50?

   b. $72?

   c. $90.40?

38. Ms. Harrison's weekly salary is $375. The payroll office withholds 17% for income tax. At the end of the year, Ms. Harrison's income tax return shows a total of $3,846 tax which should have been paid. Does Ms. Harrison owe more income tax, or does she have a refund coming, and how much?

39. Paper prices are now 1.5 times what they were three years ago. What percent increase is this?

40. A first baseman has made successful plays 85.8% of the time this season.
   a. What percent of the time has he made errors?

   b–c. He has made 168 plays so far this season.
      b. How many have been successful?

   c. How many errors has he made?

41. Last year Ms. Howard made $15,000. This year she will make $18,000.
   a. What percent of last year's salary is this year's salary?

   b. By what percent did her salary increase?

   c. What percent of this year's salary was last year's salary?

   d. By what percent was last year's salary less?

42. An artist sold 20% of the pictures he painted.
   a. He painted 50 pictures. How many did he sell?

   b. He sold 18 pictures. How many did he paint?

43.   Corbett High School's new stadium seats 3,000 people. The old stadium seated only 1,800 people. By what percent has the seating capacity increased?

44.   Of 50 attempted passes by a quarterback, 30 have been completed and 5 have been intercepted by the other team. What percent of the total number of attempted passes
       a. have been completed?

       b. have been intercepted?

       c. have not been completed?

       d. have been successful?

       e. have been unsuccessful?

45.   A foot is what percent of
       a. 1 inch?

       b. 8 inches?

       c. 24 inches?

46. Big Corporation has a suggestion box for its employees to use. The employee gets a bonus of 4% of whatever the company saves during the first year the suggestion is used. How much bonus does an employee get if his or her suggestion saves _____ during the first year it is used?

    a. $100,000

    b. $235,000

47. How much is 20% of $\frac{3}{5}$ of 600?

48. A store advertises 20% off everything inside. You go inside and buy
    a. a dryer. The regular price is $250. How much is the sale price?

    b. a refrigerator. The sale price is $360. What is the regular price?

    c. a TV set with a regular price of $425 and a microwave oven with a regular price of $305. How much do you pay (total)?

    d. a stereo set on sale for $240 and a kitchen range on sale for $450. What is the combined regular price of these two items?

49. The Carlins bought a set of storm windows for their house. They paid $100 down. They paid the balance in 12 equal payments of $78.40 each. The windows would have been a total of $940 if they had paid cash. What annual rate of interest was charged on the original unpaid balance?

50. What percent of one meter is
    a. 1 centimeter?

    b. 13 centimeters?

    c. 84 centimeters?

51. A basketball player made field goals 65% of the times she tried them.
    a. She tried to make a field goal 140 times. How many did she make?

    b. She made 104 field goals. How many times did she try?

52. A TV station received 5,000 letters about a program it showed: 65% of the writers said they liked the program; 30% said they didn't like it; 5% didn't say whether or not they liked it but complained about the commercials shown.

    a. How many said they liked the program?

    b. How many said they didn't like the program?

    c. How many complained about the commercials?

53. It was a week before the deadline for getting new license plates. On her way home from work, Ms. Elton counted 365 cars with new plates and 190 cars with old plates. To the nearest whole number, what percent of the cars she counted

    a. showed new license plates?

    b. still showed old license plates?

54. A grocer sells goods for 25% more than they cost her.

    a. What is her selling price of goods which cost her $12.60?

    b. What was her cost of goods she sold for $75?

55. What is the monthly rate of interest if the yearly rate is
    a. 12%?

    b. 18%?

    c. 10%?

56. What percent of one hour is
    a. 20 minutes?

    b. 30 minutes?

    c. 40 minutes?

57. Darwin takes 20% longer to do a job than you take.
    a. The job takes you 15 minutes. How long does it take Darwin?

    b. The job takes Darwin 45 minutes. How long does it take you?

58. Big Supermarket said its sales increased 30% during last month's advertising campaign.

    a. The sales averaged $131,287.50 before the campaign. How much did they average during the campaign?

    b. The sales averaged $146,381.82 during the campaign. How much did they average before the campaign?

59. Loretta needs to get a score of at least 70% on the next test.

    a. The test will have 20 problems. How many must she get right?

    b. She must get at least 21 problems right. How many problems will the test have?

    c. She can get no more than 12 problems wrong. How many problems will the test have?

60. The national unemployment rate is 5.4%. The "work force" is the number of people either working or looking for work.

    a. The work force is 90 million. How many people are unemployed?

    b. What is the work force if 4,064,040 people are looking for work?

61. You bought a new car a year ago for $5,800. It is now worth only $4,500.
   a. What percent of the original cost is the car now worth?

   b. What percent of the original cost has the car decreased in value?

62. There are 65,847 voters registered in the Corbett School District. At a recent school board election,
   a. only about 12.1% of the voters voted. About how many people voted?

   b. only 4,401 people voted. To the nearest tenth, what percent of the registered voters was this?

63. A sweater which sold for $15 is now on sale for $11.25. What percent discount is being given?

64. You bought some stock a year ago for $5,000. By what percent has the value decreased if the stock is now worth
   a. $4,900?

   b. $2,500?

   c. $3,000?

65.   What percent of a pound is
    a.   4 ounces?

    b.   10 ounces?

    c.   24 ounces?

66.   A jetliner carries 25% more fuel than is needed.
    a–b.   How long can the plane fly before running out of fuel if the flight normally takes
    a.   4 hours?

    b.   6 hours 40 minutes?

    c–d.   How long does the flight normally take if the plane has enough fuel to fly
    c.   6 hours?

    d.   4 hours 10 minutes?

67.   Mr. Jeffers was late getting to work a total of $6\frac{1}{2}$ hours last week. He was not allowed to make up the time lost. He was supposed to work 40 hours.
   a.   What percent of last week's time did he lose by being late?

   b.   He gets $8 an hour. How much money did he lose by being late?

68.   How much is $\frac{2}{5}$ of 70% of 300?

69.   A research laboratory reports a 65% success rate with a new method.
   a.   The method has been used 80 times. How many times has it failed?

   b.   The method has succeeded 78 times. How many times has it been used?

   c.   The method failed 224 times. How many times has it been used?

   d.   The method has succeeded 468 times. How many times has it failed?

   e.   The method has failed 126 times. How many times has it succeeded?

70. At a certain company, 12% of the workers are usually absent, and 150 people work at this company.

   a. How many workers are usually absent on a working day?

   b. Suppose the same amount of work is to get done as when everyone is working. By what percent is the workload of the remaining workers increased?

71. A 6-year savings certificate earns $7\frac{1}{2}$% annual interest. How much interest will be earned over the life of the certificate if

   a. $1,000 is invested?

   b. $7,000 is invested?

   c. $5,500 is invested?

72. For filing Form A (a tax form) late, the penalty is 5% for each 30 days (or part thereof). But the penalty cannot go over 25%. Goofers filed Form A late. There was $520 tax due on it. How much money was due for the penalty if Goofers filed the form

   a. 30 days late?

   b. 45 days late?

   c. 90 days late?

   d. 210 days late?

73.   The owner of a hardware store bought some pipe fittings for $3.50 each and sold
      them for $5 each.
      a. What percent of the selling price was the cost?

      b. What percent of the selling price was the profit?

      c. What percent of the cost was the selling price?

      d. What percent of the cost was the profit?

74.   A savings account earns 5% annual interest compounded quarterly. Ms. King put
      $3,000 in a savings account on April 1st. Each time interest was earned, she left it in
      the account. She did not add or take out any other amounts.
      a. How much was in the account on July 1st?

      b. How much was in the account on October 1st?

      c. How much was in the account on the following April 1st?

75. A candy store owner wants to sell a mixture of two kinds of candies. The first kind sells for $2 a pound. The second kind sells for $3 a pound. How much should the mixture sell for if it is made of
  a. 50% of each kind?

  b. 40% of the first kind and 60% of the second kind?

  c. 20% of the first kind and 80% of the second kind?

  d. 80% of the first kind and 20% of the second kind?

76. A credit card company charges an annual interest rate of 18% on the average unpaid balance. The interest charge is wiped out if the cardholder pays the bill by the due date.
  a. What percent is the monthly interest?

  b. The Crilons' average unpaid balance last month was $322. How much extra will they have to pay if they are late in paying the bill?

  c. In item b above, suppose the Crilons paid all but $10 by the due date. How much will the interest charge be?

77. An antiques dealer bought a chair for $500. She sold it for $800. What percent of the selling price was

    a. the profit?

    b. the cost?

78. A savings account in your bank pays 5% annual interest compounded quarterly. A savings account in your credit union pays 6% annual interest compounded quarterly. You have $6,000 to invest. Interest is rounded to the nearest cent.

    a. Make a schedule like the one below and fill it in.

End of Quarter Number	BANK		CREDIT UNION	
	Quarterly Interest	Balance	Quarterly Interest	Balance
0	0	$6000.00	0	$6000.00
1				
2				
3				
4				
5				
6				
7				
8				

    b. At which place will you have a higher balance at the end of two years, and how much higher will it be?

79.   The average American male is 5 feet 10 inches tall. Mr. Harper is 5 feet 11 inches tall. By what percent is Mr. Harper taller than the average American male?

80.   How much is $85\frac{7}{8}$ % $-\frac{3}{4}$?

81.   A sewing supplies store bought a bolt of material for $1.50 a meter and sold it for $2.25 a meter.

   a.   What percent of the selling price was the cost?

   b.   What percent of the selling price was the profit?

   c.   What percent of the cost was the selling price?

   d.   What percent of the cost was the profit?

82. A department store salesperson gets a base salary of $120 a week. Besides this, he gets 2% of all the sales he makes. How much did he make last week if his sales were
a. $537?

b. $4,887.50?

83. Refer again to problem 82 above. How much were the salesperson's sales last week if he made
a. $171.75?

b. $415.79?

84. a. Big Corporation stock sold yesterday for $70 a share. Today it is $80 a share. By what percent did the price increase?

b. Big Corporation stock sold yesterday for $80 a share. Today it is $70 a share. By what percent did the price decrease?

85. For filing Form B (a tax form) late, the penalty is 5% for each month (or part thereof). The penalty does not go over 25%. Besides the penalty, interest of $\frac{1}{2}$% a month (or part thereof) is charged. Bumblers filed Form B late. There was $3,879.45 due on it.

a–c. How much money was due for penalties if Bumblers filed Form B

    a. $1\frac{1}{2}$ months late?

    b. 5 months late?

    c. 7 months late?

d–f. How much money was due for interest if Bumblers filed Form B

    d. $1\frac{1}{2}$ months late?

    e. 5 months late?

    f. 7 months late?

g–i. How much money was due for penalties and interest if Bumblers filed Form B

    g. $1\frac{1}{2}$ months late?

    h. 5 months late?

    i. 7 months late?

86.   A gallon is what percent of
    a. 1 quart?

    b. 2 quarts?

    c. 9 quarts?

87.   You work as a car salesperson. You get a commission of 3% of the selling price. On the average, a car sells for $6,140. On this basis, how many cars do you have to sell
    a. in a week to make at least $450 that week?

    b. in a year to average at least $450 a week?

88.   Five years ago a home computer cost $990. Now the cost of such a computer is $550.
    a. What percent of the old cost is the cost now?

    b. By what percent did the cost of a home computer decrease?

    c. What percent of today's cost was the old cost?

    d. By what percent was the old cost higher than today's cost?

89.   Mark scored 80% on a test.
   a.   The test had 25 problems on it. How many problems did Mark have wrong?

   b.   Mark had 16 problems right. How many problems were on the test?

   c.   Mark had 12 problems wrong. How many problems were on the test?

90.   At Corbett High School, 45% of the students take business courses.
   a.   Corbett has 1,120 students. How many take business courses?

   b.   At Corbett, 783 students take business courses. How many students does Corbett have?

91.   A 4-year savings certificate earns 7% annual interest. A 6-year savings certificate earns 7% annual interest. You have $5,000 to invest. How much more a year will the interest be on the 6-year certificate than on the 4-year certificate?

92.   What percent of one week is
        a.   1 day?

        b.   3 days?

        c.   6 days?

93.   A survey last week showed that 47.1% of the people interviewed said they watch TV every day. Another 42.7% said they watch TV only about 3 or 4 times a week. And 15.2% said they watch TV only once a week or less. What's wrong with these results?

94.   A certain kind of candy is 63% sugar.
       a–b.   You bought 5 pounds of the candy. Answer to the nearest tenth.
         a.   How many pounds are sugar?

         b.   How many ounces are sugar?

       c–d.   Of the candy you bought, 5 pounds is sugar. Answer to the nearest tenth.
         c.   How many pounds of candy did you buy?

         d.   How many ounces of candy did you buy?

95.   A chemical is made up of six different ingredients. It contains 5 grams of A, 1.5 grams
       of B, 2 grams of C, 11.5 grams of D, 3.25 grams of E, and 1.75 grams of F. What
       percent of the mixture is
       a. A?

       b. B?

       c. C?

       d. D?

       e. E?

       f. F?

96.   Hamburger contains 26% fat. You buy 5 pounds of hamburger. When you cook it, how
       much of it
       a. will fry away as melted fat?

       b. will be left as meat to eat?

Answers

1. Introductory Word Problems

1. 30 mph
2. 50
3. 400
4. 50 km
5. 3
6. 50
7. $50
8. 4
9. $400
10. 3
11. $30
12. $400
13. $4
14. **a.** 30 years **b.** 30 years **c.** 30
15. 400 years
16. 3
17. 4
18. 50 years
19. $\frac{1}{4}$
20. 4
21. 3
22. 30 pounds
23. 400 pounds
24. 4 pounds
25. 50 pounds
26. $50
27. $30 a share
28. $400
29. 4
30. 3
31. $400
32. 50 minutes
33. 30
34. 400 minutes
35. 3
36. 50
37. 4
38. **a.** $\frac{1}{4}$ **b.** $\frac{3}{4}$
39. 30
40. 400
41. 4
42. 30
43. 50
44. 4 meters
45. **a.** $\frac{1}{4}$ **b.** $\frac{3}{4}$ **c.** 3
46. 30 meters
47. 400 meters
48. $400
49. $30
50. $50
51. $4
52. $400
53. 3
54. 3
55. 30
56. 4
57. 50
58. 4
59. 400
60. 3
61. $30 a case
62. 3
63. $50

2. Decimals

1. $10.87 (Note: As indicated in instruction E on page 106, gasoline charges are figured from pump readings, and these readings are usually taken as shown—i.e., rounded in the usual arithmetic methods.)
2. $6.53
3. 5.75
4. 56 minutes
5. 25 minutes
6. $193.17
7. **a.** .300 **b.** .364 **c.** .316
8. **a.** .5 pounds
   b. 1.06$\frac{1}{4}$ pounds
   c. 121.6 ounces
9. 36¢
10. **a.** $21,850.92
    b. $1,820.91
11. $3.35
12. 1.44 meters
13. $3.39
14. **a.** $13.29 **b.** $2.03
15. 1.29$\frac{39}{209}$
16. $27.55
17. 2.16$\frac{104}{231}$
18. $37.36
19. The first dealer's price was $237.81 higher.
20. 8.55 cm
21. **a.** .75 feet
    b. .66$\frac{2}{3}$ feet
    c. 40.8 inches
22. **a.** $1.75 **b.** $1.12
    c. $2.87 **d.** $7.13
23. 5.3
24. $360.58
25. $21,598.20
26. **a.** $14.06 **b.** $14.24
27. **a.** $28.41 **b.** $9.47
    c. $1.59
28. $36.74
29. **a.** $57,703.50
    b. $51,903.50
30. $5.87
31. 1.28$\frac{136}{1835}$
32. **a.** $14,924.52
    b. $287.01
33. **a.** .75 years
    b. 1.41$\frac{2}{3}$ years
    c. 140.4 months
34. 12¢
35. $9.72
36. **a.** 1,975 **b.** 1,264

37. 3

38. .5 cm

39. 10.6 cm

40. 13.4 cm

41. It totals 1.05 of the income. In other words, it accounts for spending more than they earn.

42. 519.2

43. **a.** $58 **b.** $43.50 **c.** $442.25

44. 2,045,319

45. 30

46. 178.125 square feet

47. 152.375 square feet

48. $11.02\frac{16}{17}$

49. 15 mpg

50. **a.** .25 hours **b.** $1.33\frac{1}{3}$ hours **c.** 165 minutes

51. $5.55\frac{7}{10}$

52. $33.33\frac{1}{3}$

53. $4.05

54. $33.95

55. **a.** 1.6 **b.** 3.4 **c.** $2.17\frac{11}{17}$

56. $36,144.75

57. 51¢

58. **a.** $1.07 **b.** $1.54 **c.** 19 minutes

59. **a.** $206.75 **b.** $895.91\frac{2}{3}$

60. **a.** .75 years **b.** $1.44\frac{3}{13}$ years **c.** 270.4 weeks

61. 204.14 miles

62. $28.47\frac{1}{17}$

63. .0678, .12, .2079, .275, .3

64. **a.** 6.75 **b.** 3.00 **c.** 3.75 **d.** 0.00

65. 3.75

66. $478.40

67. $6.36\frac{2}{3}$

68. $15.97\frac{1}{2}$ cm

69. **a.** $7,760,954.75 **b.** $3,256,892.10

70. **a.** $87.20 **b.** $261.60

71. $1.98\frac{46}{73}$

72. 482.5 kph

73. **a.** $.71\frac{3}{7}$ weeks **b.** $2.42\frac{6}{7}$ weeks **c.** 28.7 days

74. .7

75. **a.** $47.05 **b.** $32.70 **c.** $14.35

76. **a.** $11,337.15 **b.** $3,687.40

77. **a.** 3.75 **b.** $13.12\frac{1}{2}$ **c.** .75 **d.** $1.12\frac{1}{2}$

78. **a.** $258.72 **b.** $21.56

79. 49¢

80. **a.** .75 gallon **b.** 4.25 gallons **c.** 18 quarts

81. **a.** 2.429 **b.** 2.000 **c.** 3.667 **d.** 3.333

82. 1.4 cm

83. **a.** 2,510,534 **b.** 122,156

84. **a.** 446 **b.** 56 **c.** 73 **d.** 89

85. 6 mph

86. 1097.46 miles

87. 54.4

88. 9.3 cm

89. **a.** $3,768.35 **b.** $4,564.80 **c.** $126.80

90. **a.** 640 **b.** 832

91. 3.94

92. **a.** $4.41\frac{2}{3}$ hours **b.** $39.85\frac{5}{7}$ weeks **c.** $.76\frac{32}{73}$ year

93. **a.** 86.2 **b.** 86 **c.** 91

94. 41 cm long and 25 cm wide

95. 800 kph

96. $7.27

97. **a.** 141.75 **b.** 453.6

c. $2.82\frac{106}{567}$

d. $11.65\frac{65}{189}$

98. $228.27

99. **a.** $4.25 **b.** $4.25 **c.** $5.75 **d.** $2.75 **e.** $4.25

100. $7\frac{1}{2}$ hours or 7.5 hours

101. **a.** $1,315.21 **b.** $1,475.04 **c.** $122.92

102. **a.** .45 m **b.** 2.67 m **c.** 187 cm

103. 36

104. **a.** 13 liters **b.** 16.25 ml **c.** $1.53\frac{11}{13}$ ml

105. **a.** $13.02 **b.** $6.98

106. **a.** $237.50 **b.** $778.45 **c.** $75

107. **a.** 30.48 **b.** 91.44 **c.** $.39\frac{47}{127}$ **d.** $1.18\frac{14}{127}$

108. $5.07

109. **a.** 8 **b.** 88 **c.** 91

110. **a.** 1.25 feet high, 1.5 feet wide, 2.25 feet long **b.** 4.21875

111. **a.** 48 **b.** 88 **c.** 80 **d.** $.62\frac{1}{2}$ **e.** 62.5 **f.** 31.25

112. 3.354 square cm

113. 1.5625 square inches

114. **a.** $.07\frac{1}{2}$ km **b.** $1.77\frac{3}{5}$ km **c.** 3,250 m

115. $5.93

116. 14.33 cm

117. 22.7 liters

118. 2.5957 cm or $2.59\frac{57}{100}$ cm

119. $3

120. 144.5

121. 10.15 cm

122. $86.02\frac{14}{93}$ kph

123. 241.68 miles

124. a. 11.355 b. 17.411
c. .26 $\frac{318}{757}$ d. 1.32 $\frac{76}{757}$
e. 1.05 $\frac{515}{757}$
f. 4.22 $\frac{546}{757}$
g. More than
125. 15 mph
126. 12.6 mpg
127. a. $122 b. $116.20

3. Percents 1

1. $273.60
2. $4,315
3. 7%
4. $1,200
5. $30,000
6. 15%
7. $305.20
8. $4,120
9. 4%
10. a. $\frac{2}{3}$ % b. 2%
11. $280
12. 9%
13. $7,500
14. a. 40 b. 15% c. 6
15. a. 90% b. 90% c. 4
d. 10%
16. a. 16% b. 21 c. 4
d. 625% e. 525%
f. 16%
17. a. $140 b. 2% c. 98%
18. a. 97% b. $6,800
c. 103 $\frac{9}{97}$ % d. $204
19. a. $225 b. $150
c. $75 d. 1%; yes
e. 97% f. $7,275
g. 98% h. $7,350
i. yes ($75)
20. a. 75% b. 25%
21. a. $\frac{1}{5}$ b. $\frac{4}{5}$
22. a. 80% b. 125%
c. 20% d. 25%
23. a. 125% b. 16 mpg
c. 80% d. 20%
24. a. 10% b. 20%
c. 30% d. 40%

e. 50% **f.** 90%
25. a. 120% b. 24 mpg
c. 83 $\frac{1}{3}$ % d. 20%
26. a. $360 b. 9% c. 18%
27. a. 100% b. 100%
c. 100% d. 100%
e. 100% f. 100%
28. a. 22% b. 11%
29. a. $400 b. $800
c. $1,200 d. $1,600
e. $200 f. $600
g. $1,000 h. $1,400
30. a. $520 b. $6,500
31. 12%
32. a. $64.13 b. 103%
c. 3%
33. a. $4,438.50
b. $177.54
34. $184.64
35. a. 66 $\frac{2}{3}$ % b. 150%
c. 50%
36. a. 125% b. $12,500
c. 80%
37. a. 112% b. $18,750
c. 89 $\frac{2}{7}$ %
38. 56
39. 106
40. a. 110% b. 55
41. a. 110% b. 60
c. 90 $\frac{10}{11}$ %
42. a. 125% b. 25%
c. 80%
43. a. 75% b. $20
c. 100% d. 133 $\frac{1}{3}$ %
e. 133 $\frac{1}{3}$ % f. 75%
44. a. $\frac{3}{2}$ b. $\frac{1}{2}$
45. a. $3.75 b. $11.25
c. 75% d. 133 $\frac{1}{3}$ %
46. a. 60% b. 40%
c. 40% d. 166 $\frac{2}{3}$ %
47. a. 75% b. 75%
c. 75% d. 75%
e. 75% f. 75%
48. a. 85% b. 117 $\frac{11}{17}$ %
c. 15%

49. a. 1000% b. 10%
c. 90%
50. .18 cm thick
51. .22 cm thick
52. a. 80% b. 20%
53. a. $75 b. $425
c. 85% d. $75
54. a. 86% b. $450
c. 116 $\frac{12}{43}$ %
55. 33 $\frac{1}{3}$ %
56. a. 16¢ b. 84¢ c. 13¢
d. $3.36 e. 25%
f. $2.52 g. 75%
57. a. $\frac{19}{20}$ b. $\frac{1}{20}$
58. a. 152 b. 114
59. a. 75% b. 25%
60. a. 30% b. 70%
61. a. 48 b. 102
62. a. $15,000 b. $35,000
c. 70% d. 30%
e. 42 $\frac{6}{7}$ %
63. a. 70% b. $60,000
c. 142 $\frac{6}{7}$ %
d. $18,000
64. a. 20% b. 40%
c. 60% d. 80%
65. a. 150% b. $2,250
66. $4,050
67. a. 140% b. $760
c. 40% d. 71 $\frac{3}{7}$ %
68. a. $\frac{9}{4}$ b. $\frac{5}{4}$ c. $\frac{1}{4}$
69. a. 25% b. 75% c. $10
d. $30
70. a. $40 b. 25% c. 75%
d. 75% e. 133 $\frac{1}{3}$ %
71. a. $12 b. $28 c. 70%
d. 142 $\frac{6}{7}$ %
72. a. 28 minutes
b. 140% c. 71 $\frac{3}{7}$ %
73. a. 140% b. 18 min.
c. 40%
74. a. 140%
b. 35 minutes
c. 14 minutes
d. 40%

75. a. 125 % b. 25%
    c. 80%
76. a. 80% b. 20 psi
77. a. 104% b. 25 psi
78. a. 18 or $\frac{18}{1}$ b. $\frac{9}{5}$
    c. $\frac{9}{50}$ d. $\frac{9}{500}$
79. a. 125% b. $10,000
    c. 25% d. 80%
80. a. $4,400 b. $48,400
    c. 110% d. $90\frac{10}{11}$ %
81. a. 70 or $\frac{70}{1}$ b. 7
    c. $\frac{7}{10}$ d. $\frac{7}{100}$
    e. $\frac{7}{1000}$
82. a. 110% b. $40,000
    c. $4,000 d. 10%
83. a. $570 b. 40%
    c. $380
84. a. 40% b. $860
    c. $516
85. a. $10 b. $2 c. $28
86. a. $20 b. $40 c. 80%
    d. $50 e. $70
87. a. 200% b. 300%
    c. 400% d. 500%
    e. 1100% f. 25,100%
    g. 389,700%
88. a. 25% b. $24 c. $18
89. a. $5 b. $15 c. 75%
90. a. 40% b. 60%
    c. $7.50
91. a. 50% b. $5 c. 200%
92. $4.30
93. a. $3.60 b. 60%
    c. 40%

4. Percents 2

1. 6 years
2. a. 50% b. 75%
   c. $83\frac{1}{3}$ %
3. a. 65% b. 35%
4. a. 741 b. 39
5. 94.9%
6. $6,489.60
7. a. $110 b. $121

c. $133.10 d. $146.41
   e. $88 f. $29.70
8. $22.72 (Note: You
   may have to point out
   that a payroll office
   rounds such amounts
   to the nearest cent.)
9. a. 200% b. $66\frac{2}{3}$ %
   c. 50%
10. a. $16,632 b. 8%
11. a. $1,320 b. $1,080
    c. $1,260 d. $1,206
    e. $1,196.40 f. $1,800
12. 6
13. a. $63 b. $85.50
    c. $99.90
14. a. $1,458.20
    b. $4,881.80
15. a. $33\frac{1}{3}$ %
    b. $66\frac{2}{3}$ %
16. 28.8%
17. a. $3 b. $300
    c. $2,557.50
18. $14,624
19. a. $12,000 b. She got
    nothing.
20. a. 50% b. 5% c. 45%
21. a. 20% b. 4% c. 2%
    d. 100%
22. a. $8\frac{1}{3}$ % b. 25%
    c. $66\frac{2}{3}$ %
23. $16.45
24. a. $50.40 b. $68.75
25. a. 25% b. 20%
26. a. $1,200 b. $1,320
    c. $1,452 d. $15,972
27. a. $280 b. $840
28. 75%
29. a. 2,460 b. 8,240
    c. 8,525
30. a. $9.45 b. $16.80
31. a. $244.20 b. $315
32. a. $1.20 b. $1.44,
    usually rounded to
    $1.50 c. $3.75

33. a. $1 b. $1.35
34. a. 24 b. 110
35. a. 25% b. 100%
    c. 250%
36. a. $107\frac{9}{13}$ %
    b. $7\frac{9}{13}$ %
    c. $92\frac{6}{7}$ % d. $7\frac{1}{7}$ %
37. a. $12\frac{1}{2}$ % b. 18%
    c. $22\frac{3}{5}$ %
38. She owes $531.
39. 50%
40. a. 14.2% b. 144 c. 24
41. a. 120% b. 20%
    c. $83\frac{1}{3}$ %
    d. $16\frac{2}{3}$ %
42. a. 10 b. 90
43. $66\frac{2}{3}$ %
44. a. 60% b. 10%
    c. 30% d. 60%
    e. 40%
45. a. 1200% b. 150%
    c. 50%
46. a. $4,000 b. $9,400
47. 72
48. a. $200 b. $450
    c. $584 d. $862.50
49. 12%
50. a. 1% b. 13% c. 84%
51. a. 91 b. 160
52. a. 3,250 b. 1,500
    c. 250
53. a. 66% b. 34%
54. a. $15.75 b. $60
55. a. 1% b. $1\frac{1}{2}$ %
    c. $\frac{5}{6}$ %
56. a. $33\frac{1}{3}$ % b. 50%
    c. $66\frac{2}{3}$ %
57. a. 18 minutes
    b. $37\frac{1}{2}$ minutes
58. a. $170,673.75
    b. $112,601.40
59. a. 14 b. 30 c. 40
60. a. 4,860,000
    b. 75,260,000 people
61. a. $77\frac{17}{29}$ %

b. $12\frac{12}{29}$ %

62. **a.** 7,967 **b.** $6\frac{7}{10}$ % or 6.7%

63. 25%

64. **a.** 2% **b.** 50% **c.** 40%

65. **a.** 25% **b.** $62\frac{1}{2}$ % **c.** 150%

66. **a.** 5 hours
b. 8 hours 20 minutes
c. 4 hours 48 minutes
d. 3 hours 20 minutes

67. **a.** $16\frac{1}{4}$ % **b.** $52

68. 84

69. **a.** 28 **b.** 120 **c.** 640
d. 252 **e.** 234

70. **a.** 18 **b.** $13\frac{7}{11}$ %

71. **a.** $450 **b.** $3,150
c. $2,475

72. **a.** $26 **b.** $52 **c.** $78
d. $130

73. **a.** 70% **b.** 30%
c. $142\frac{6}{7}$ %
d. $42\frac{6}{7}$ %

74. **a.** $3,037.50
b. $3,075.47
c. $3,152.83

75. **a.** $2.50 a pound
b. $2.60 a pound
c. $2.80 a pound
d. $2.20 a pound

76. **a.** $1\frac{1}{2}$ % **b.** $4.83
c. $4.83 (Note: Such charges are made on the average unpaid balance unless the entire bill is paid. An exception is made if an amount is unpaid because of a dispute in billing.)

77. **a.** $37\frac{1}{2}$ %
b. $62\frac{1}{2}$ %

78. **a.** See table at right
b. It will be $132.04 higher at the credit

union.

79. $1\frac{3}{7}$ %

80. $10\frac{7}{8}$ %

81. **a.** $66\frac{2}{3}$ %
b. $33\frac{1}{3}$ %
c. 150% **d.** 50%

82. **a.** $130.74 **b.** $217.75

83. **a.** $2,587.50
b. $14,789.50

84. **a.** $14\frac{2}{7}$ %
b. $12\frac{1}{2}$ %

85. **a.** $387.95
b. $969.86
c. $969.86
d. $38.79
e. $96.99
f. $135.78
g. $426.74
h. $1,066.85
i. $1,105.64

86. **a.** 400% **b.** 200%
c. $44\frac{4}{9}$ %

87. **a.** 3 (Note: You may have to point out to

your students that it is not possible to sell just part of a new car.) **b.** 128

88. **a.** $55\frac{5}{9}$ %
b. $44\frac{4}{9}$ %
c. 180%
d. 80%

89. **a.** 5 **b.** 20 **c.** 60

90. **a.** 504 **b.** 1,740

91. $37.50

92. **a.** $14\frac{2}{7}$ %
b. $42\frac{6}{7}$ %
c. $85\frac{5}{7}$ %

93. They total over 100%. (Ask your students why such a result is not possible.)

94. **a.** 3.2 **b.** 50.4 **c.** 7.9
d. 127.0

95. **a.** 20% **b.** 6% **c.** 8%
d. 46% **e.** 13% **f.** 7%

96. **a.** 1.3 pounds
b. 3.7 pounds

78. a.

End of Quarter Number	BANK		CREDIT UNION	
	Quarterly Interest	Balance	Quarterly Interest	Balance
0	0	$6000.00	0	$6000.00
1	$75.00	6,075.00	$90.00	6,090.00
2	75.94	6,150.94	91.35	6,181.35
3	76.89	6,227.83	92.72	6,274.07
4	77.85	6,305.68	94.11	6,368.18
5	78.82	6,384.50	95.52	6,463.70
6	79.81	6,464.31	96.96	6,560.66
7	80.80	6,545.11	98.41	6,659.07
8	81.81	6,626.92	99.89	6,758.96